LIFE CYCLES
Tulips

by Melanie Mitchell

Lerner Publications Company · Minneapolis

This is a **tulip**.

A tulip is a flower, like a
daisy or a rose.

There are many kinds of
tulips.

How do tulips grow?

Tulips grow from **bulbs**.

A bulb is planted in the fall.

Right away, the bulb
grows **roots**.

The bulb stops growing
when winter comes.

In the spring, the bulb
starts growing again.

A **shoot** appears
above the ground.

The shoot grows bigger.

Next a tulip **bud** appears.

One day, the bud opens
into a tulip.

Some people cut the tulips
to put inside.

Others enjoy tulips outside.

Next spring, a new tulip will
grow from the same bulb.

Life Cycle of a Tulip

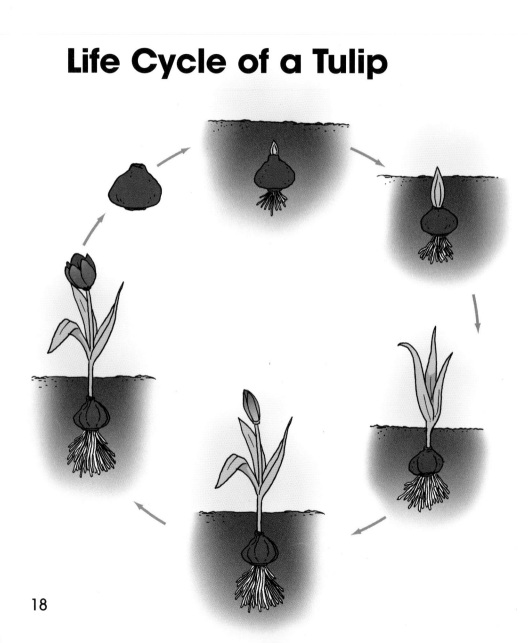

How to Grow Tulips

1. Buy tulip bulbs that are firm and have no cuts or mold on them.
2. In the fall, dig a 6-inch hole and plant a tulip bulb with the pointed end facing up. Tulip bulbs should be planted 5 inches apart.
3. After planting, pat down the soil on top. Water well.
4. Do not water again until the shoots appear in the spring.
5. Your tulip bulb will follow the life cycle shown on page 18.

Tulip Facts

 Tulips did not come from Holland, as most people think. They came from Central Asia. The word *tulip* is thought to have come from the Turkish word for turban.

 Holland is now the tulip capital of the world. More tulips grow there than anywhere else.

 "Tulip Mania" happened in the 1600s. People sometimes traded everything they owned for a single tulip bulb.

The Canadian Tulip Festival is the world's largest tulip festival. It is held in May in Ottawa, Canada. Millions of tulips are planted, and people come from all over the world to see them.

 Tulips come in every color except blue and true black.

 Tulip petals are said to taste like sweet lettuce.

Glossary

 bud – a flower that has not opened yet

 bulbs – plant parts that can grow new plants

 roots – parts of a plant that grow down into the soil

 shoot – part of a plant that has just started to grow

 tulip – a plant with colorful flowers that grows from a bulb

Index

The photographs in this book are reproduced through the courtesy of: © Richard Daybreak/ Daybreak Imagery, front cover, p. 14; Netherlands Flower Bulb Information Center, pp. 2, 6, 7, 16, 22 (second from top, bottom); © Diane Cooper, p. 3; © Dwight Kuhn, pp. 4, 8, 22 (middle); © Todd Strand/Independent Picture Service, pp. 5, 9, 10, 13, 22 (top); © Renee Weddle/ Independent Picture Service, pp. 11, 12, 15, 17, 22 (second from bottom).

Illustration page 18 by Tim Seeley.

Lerner Publishing Company
A division of Lerner Publishing Group
241 First Avenue North
Minneapolis, MN 55401 USA

Website address: www.lernerbooks.com

Library of Congress Cataloging-in-Publication Data

Mitchell, Melanie S.
    Tulips / by Melanie Mitchell.
        p.   cm. — (First step nonfiction) (Life cycles.)
    Summary: A basic overview of the life cycle of a tulip.
    ISBN: 0–8225–4614–0 (lib. bdg. : alk. paper)
    1. Tulips—Life cycles—Juvenile literature. [1. Tulips.]
I. Title. II. Series.
SB413.T9 M48 2003
635.9'3432—dc21   2002004872

Manufactured in the United States of America
1 2 3 4 5 6 – JR – 08 07 06 05 04 03

10/03